P9-DGB-646

Science Experiments

Experiments
You Can Do
in Your Backyard

WATERBIRD BOOKS

Columbus, Ohio

President: Vincent F. Douglas

Publisher: Tracey E. Dils

Project Editors: Joanna Callihan and Nathan Hemmelgarn

Contributors: Q.L. Pearce, Barbara Saffer, Ph.D., Sophie Sheppard,

Leo Abbett, and Neal Yamamoto

Art Directors: Robert Sanford and Christopher Fowler

Interior Design and Production: Jennifer Bowers

Cover Design: Jennifer Bowers

The Academic Standards e-Library

This product has been aligned to state and national organization standards using the Align to Achieve Standards Database. Align to Achieve, Inc., is an independent, not-for-profit organization that facilitates the evaluation and improvement of academic standards and student achievement. To find how this product aligns to your standards, go to www.MHstandards.com.

Children's Publishing

This edition published in the United States of America in 2003 by Waterbird Books,
an imprint of McGraw-Hill Children's Publishing,
a Division of The McGraw-Hill Companies
8787 Orion Place
Columbus, Ohio 43240-4027

www.MHkids.com

Library of Congress Cataloging-in-Publication Data is on file with the publisher.

Printed in the United States of America.

1-57768-624-1

1 2 3 4 5 6 7 8 9 10 PHXBK 09 08 07 06 05 04 03

Experiments You Can Do in Your Backyard

Contents

<table>
<tr><td>• Getting Started in the Backyard</td><td>4</td><td>• Putt-Putt Power</td><td>52</td></tr>
<tr><td>• Stay Cool</td><td>5</td><td>• Quick Quicksand</td><td>54</td></tr>
<tr><td>• Temperature Test</td><td>6</td><td>• Let it Snow</td><td>56</td></tr>
<tr><td>• Drip Drop</td><td>8</td><td>• Keeping Warm</td><td>58</td></tr>
<tr><td>• Here Comes the Sun</td><td>10</td><td>• Earth to Star</td><td>60</td></tr>
<tr><td>• Shadow Art</td><td>12</td><td>• No Question North</td><td>62</td></tr>
<tr><td>• Spinning Wheel</td><td>14</td><td>• Fountain Fun</td><td>64</td></tr>
<tr><td>• Tricky Wind</td><td>16</td><td>• Water Loss</td><td>66</td></tr>
<tr><td>• Invisible Push</td><td>17</td><td>• Changing Colors</td><td>67</td></tr>
<tr><td>• Some Like it Dark</td><td>18</td><td>• Snip and Clip</td><td>68</td></tr>
<tr><td>• Fantastic Funnel</td><td>20</td><td>• Going Green</td><td>70</td></tr>
<tr><td>• Ant Bait</td><td>22</td><td>• Reach for the Light</td><td>72</td></tr>
<tr><td>• Wild Webs</td><td>24</td><td>• Washing Away</td><td>74</td></tr>
<tr><td>• Along Came a Spider</td><td>26</td><td>• Dig Deep</td><td>76</td></tr>
<tr><td>• Free, Fresh Air</td><td>27</td><td>• Sandy Swing</td><td>78</td></tr>
<tr><td>• Dinner Guests</td><td>28</td><td>• Can Contest</td><td>80</td></tr>
<tr><td>• Keeping Track</td><td>30</td><td>• Whirl and Twirl</td><td>82</td></tr>
<tr><td>• The Better to See You With</td><td>32</td><td>• Volcano</td><td>84</td></tr>
<tr><td>• Direction Reflection</td><td>33</td><td>• Before and After</td><td>85</td></tr>
<tr><td>• Any Way the Wind Blows</td><td>34</td><td>• Left or Right</td><td>86</td></tr>
<tr><td>• The Air Down Under</td><td>36</td><td>• On Target</td><td>87</td></tr>
<tr><td>• Soil's Secret</td><td>37</td><td>• Rain Rates</td><td>88</td></tr>
<tr><td>• Wonderful Water</td><td>38</td><td>• Hair and Humidity</td><td>90</td></tr>
<tr><td>• No Sweat</td><td>40</td><td>• Bubbling Rock</td><td>93</td></tr>
<tr><td>• Down with Detergents</td><td>41</td><td>• Don't Crowd Me</td><td>94</td></tr>
<tr><td>• Tea Garden</td><td>42</td><td>• Jiminy Cricket</td><td>96</td></tr>
<tr><td>• A Change In the Weather</td><td>43</td><td></td><td></td></tr>
<tr><td>• A Recipe for Dirt</td><td>44</td><td></td><td></td></tr>
<tr><td>• Down the Drain</td><td>46</td><td></td><td></td></tr>
<tr><td>• Earthworks</td><td>47</td><td></td><td></td></tr>
<tr><td>• Number the Stars</td><td>48</td><td></td><td></td></tr>
<tr><td>• Spinning Fountain</td><td>50</td><td></td><td></td></tr>
</table>

Getting Started in the Backyard

What is soil made of? Do plants breathe? What do snails eat? The answers to these questions and more are as near as your own backyard. With a few simple materials, you can set up your own weather station, start a spider web collection, or count the stars in the night sky.

Here are some basic safety tips:

- Before you begin, read the directions completely.
- Wear old clothing or an apron.
- Never put an unknown material into your mouth or near your eyes.
- Ask permission before digging any holes.
- Be careful not to harm living things.
- Clean your work area when you are finished.
- Wash your hands when you are finished.

Most of the materials you will need for these experiments are probably already in your home. Check with an adult before you use any household supplies. You may need an adult helper for some of the experiments in this book.

Stay Cool

Desert animals have different methods of staying cool. Some are active at night when the air temperature is cooler than in the daytime. Some animals spend the day in an underground burrow. This experiment will show why that strategy works.

Materials

- small garden spade
- 2 outdoor thermometers
- notebook
- pencil

Directions

❶ In a shady spot, check the temperature of both thermometers to be sure that they match. Record the temperature in your notebook.

❷ In a sunny spot, where it's okay to dig, dig a 6-inch-deep hole in the soil large enough to hold one thermometer.

❸ Bury the first thermometer in the hole, covering it lightly with dirt. Lay the other thermometer on the top of the soil facing the sun.

❹ After 10 minutes, record the temperature of the thermometer in the sun. Quickly dig up the buried thermometer and record the temperature.

Action, Reaction, Results

The earth is heated by the rays of the sun. The buried thermometer is shielded from the sun's direct rays by a layer of soil. It does not get as hot as the other thermometer. Desert animals can also find shelter from the sun by burrowing under the soil where it is cooler.

Temperature Test

Suppose you place a block of wood and an ice cube on a sunny windowsill and wait for the temperature of each to rise by 1 degree. The temperature of the block of wood rises faster than the temperature of the ice cube. In other words, more heat is needed to warm up ice than wood. Scientists say ice has higher heat capacity than wood.

Materials

- two identical empty cans
- soil
- water
- two outdoor thermometers
- pencil
- sheet of paper
- watch or clock
- shady spot
- hot, sunny spot

Directions

❶ Get two identical empty cans. Fill one with soil and one with water.

❷ Put an outdoor thermometer into each can. Leave both cans in a shady spot for a few hours, so that the soil and water reach the same temperature. Record the temperature on a piece of paper.

❸ Place both cans in a hot, sunny place.

❹ Check and record the temperatures of the soil and the water every 15 minutes for 2 hours. Which substance warms up faster, soil or water?

Action, Reaction, Results

The soil heated up more quickly than the water. This happened because more heat is needed to warm up water than soil. Scientists say water has higher "heat capacity" than soil. In fact, water has higher heat capacity than most common substances.

Something Extra
Make a frosty foot. Get a pair of white socks. Soak one sock in water and wring it out. Go outside and put the wet sock on one bare foot and the dry sock on the other bare foot. Sit with your feet out in sunlight. Does one foot feel cooler than the other? Why do you think this is?

Drip Drop

You may not always see it, but there is water hidden in many places in our environment. With a few simple supplies and a warm day, you can build your own moisture trap.

Materials

- small shovel
- margarine container
- 2-foot-square sheet of plastic (such as painter's tarp)
- 4 large rocks
- several small pebbles

Directions

❶ Start this experiment on a warm, sunny day. Find a spot in your yard where it is okay to dig. Dig a cone-shaped hole about 18 inches across at the top, 6 inches across at the bottom, and 1 foot deep.

❷ Place an open, empty margarine container at the bottom of the hole.

❸ Spread the plastic sheet out flat over the hole and secure it at each corner with a rock.

❹ Pile the pebbles in the center of the plastic so that the plastic sags toward the margarine container.

❺ Leave everything in place overnight. Check the margarine container for moisture the following morning.

Action, Reaction, Results

Soil, even desert soil, contains some water. The air contains water, too. Water from lakes, rivers, and other sources evaporates into the air and becomes water vapor. In your experiment, the warmth of the sun causes water in the soil to evaporate. Warm air holds more water vapor than cold air. As the air cools at night, condensation forms on the plastic. Drops of water roll down the plastic and drip into the container at the bottom of the hole.

WORD FILE

- **Condensation:** Liquid formed by cooling a vapor.
- **Evaporate:** To change liquid into a vapor using heat or moving air.

Something Extra

Building a moisture trap can be a lifesaver for someone lost in a desert when even a small drink of water can make a difference.

Here Comes the Sun

You can tell time without a watch by building this solar timepiece in your backyard.

Materials

- stiff cardboard
- ruler
- pencil
- scissors
- lid to a cardboard shoe box at least 6 inches wide
- protractor 6 inches high
- compass
- watch

Directions

1. Prepare your sundial early in the morning or the night before you intend to mark it. Draw a triangle on the stiff cardboard. It must have two 6-inch sides at a right angle to each other. The third side will be about 8 inches long. At the base of the triangle, draw a $\frac{1}{2}$-inch-wide strip, as shown.

2. Cut out the triangle and strip in one piece to form a triangle with a $\frac{1}{2}$-inch tab at the base.

3. Use the protractor to draw a semicircle on the top of the shoe box lid, as shown. Draw a line across the width of the lid at the center. Cut a slit along the line. Slip the tab of the triangle into the slit so that the triangle stands up straight and at a right angle to the lid.

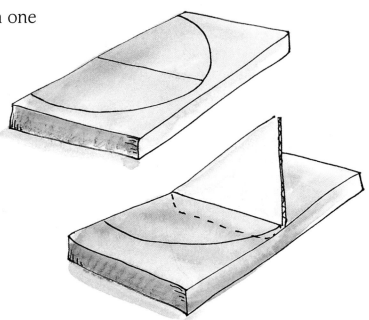

❹ With the triangle pointing north and south, place the lid in a location that's sunny all day.

❺ Begin early in the morning. On the hour, make a line on the lid where the shadow falls and write the hour at that mark. Repeat the process every hour marking the hours until sundown.

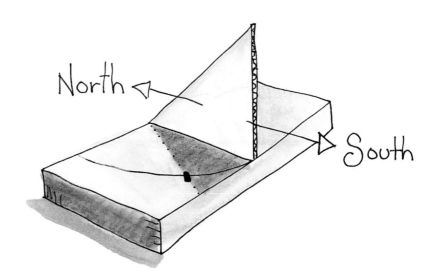

Action, Reaction, Results

The triangle on your sundial is called a gnomon. The angle of the shadow that it casts depends on the position of the sun. The sun appears to move across the sky from east to west in a path called the ecliptic. As it completes its daily journey, the angle on the sundial changes hour to hour, but the pattern is the same each day. Once you have marked your sundial, you will be able to use it to tell the time whenever the sun is up.

WORD FILE

- **Angle:** The area between two lines that meet. An angle is measured in degrees.
- **Ecliptic:** The sun's apparent path through the sky relative to the stars.
- **Gnomon:** The raised portion of a sundial that casts a shadow.

Something Extra
The earliest known sundial is from Egypt, and it is three thousand years old!

Shadow Art

A shadow is a patch of shade formed by an object that blocks lamplight or sunlight. On a sunny day, many outdoor objects cast shadows. The shadows change in size and shape over the course of the day.

Materials

- sunny day
- sidewalk or driveway exposed to sunlight
- large sheet of paper
- object with an interesting shape (like a small watering can)
- colored markers
- clock or watch

Directions

❶ On a sunny morning, find a place on a sidewalk or driveway that's exposed to sunlight and not in the way of people or cars. Put down a large piece of paper.

❷ Place an object with an interesting shape, like a small watering can, in the middle of the paper.

❸ Use a colored marker to trace around the object's shadow. Look at a clock or watch, and record the time beside the drawing.

❹ Wait 1 hour, then trace the object's shadow again, using a different color marker. Record the time beside the second drawing.

❺ Continue to trace the object's shadow every hour, using a different color marker each time. Record the time for each drawing. Try to make six to eight drawings. How does the shadow change over the course of the day?

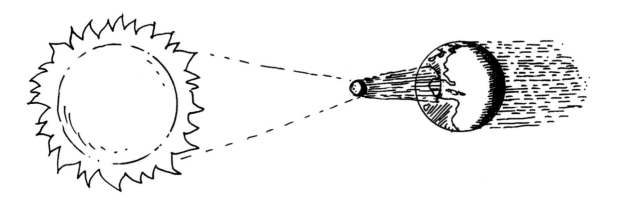

Action, Reaction, Results

Each time you drew the object, its shadow was different. The shadow changed because the position of the sun changed. The earth *revolves,* or turns completely around, once per day. When a part of the earth faces the sun, it's daytime in that area. When a part of the earth faces away from the sun, it's nighttime in that area. Because the earth turns, the sun appears to rise, move across the sky, and set every day. When the sun is low in the sky, at sunrise and sunset, shadows are long and thin. When the sun is high in the sky, at midday, shadows are short and thick.

Something Extra

Take a shadow stroll. Ask an adult to take a walk with you in the late afternoon. Since the sun is low in the sky, shadows will be long. Can you make your shadow go around corners of buildings or zigzag up stairs? Look at shadows of different things. Do any of them look like cars? trucks? animals? vegetables? other things?

Spinning Wheel

In this experiment, absorption and reflection of heat are made to do work.

Materials

- two 1- by 2-inch strips of stiff poster board
- aluminum foil
- scissors
- black paint and paintbrush
- glue
- 5 inches of lightweight thread
- pencil
- glass jar at least 3 inches wide

Directions

❶ Cover the poster board strips with aluminum foil.

❷ Cut a $\frac{1}{2}$-inch vertical slit in the center of each strip. Turn one strip over and slip the two slit sides together to form a paddle wheel.

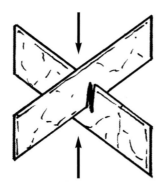

❸ Paint the "back" side of each paddle black and let the paint dry. When you turn the wheel toward you, you should see the foil-covered surface. As you turn it away, you should see the black painted surface.

❹ Glue one end of the thread to the top center of the wheel.

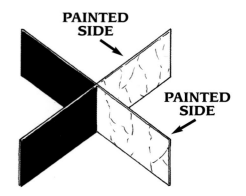

PAINTED SIDE

PAINTED SIDE

❺ Lay the pencil across the top of the open jar. Tie the loose end of the thread around the center of the pencil so that the wheel hangs freely in the center of the jar. Place the jar in a very sunny spot and observe.

Action, Reaction, Results

Within minutes, the wheel begins to turn. The dark surfaces of the wheel absorb much more heat from the Sun than the shiny surfaces do. Sunlight is actually reflected away from the shiny sides of the wheel. This uneven heating and radiated energy cause the wheel to turn.

Something Extra
How much more heat is absorbed by a dark surface? Place two outdoor thermometers side by side in a sunny window. Lay a piece of black paper over one and white paper over the other. Wait 15 minutes and check the temperature of each thermometer. Which thermometer registers a higher temperature?

Tricky Wind

Have you ever watched the wind tossing the leaves of a tree? Does the wind travel in a straight line, or can it go around corners? Here's a way to find out.

Materials

- small stick about 6 inches long
- tissue paper
- scissors
- clear tape
- golf ball-sized lump of clay
- $\frac{1}{2}$-liter soda bottle

Directions

❶ Cut a strip of tissue paper about 2 inches long and about an inch wide. Make a series of small inch-long slits at one end. Tape the uncut end around one end of the stick.

❷ On a flat surface, push the other end of the stick into the clay so that it stands up straight. Place the bottle next to the stick, leaving about $\frac{1}{2}$ inch of space between them.

❸ Position yourself so you are at eye level with the bottle on the opposite side from the stick. With the bottle between you and the stick, blow toward the top of the stick. Does the tissue paper flutter?

Action, Reaction, Results

Air flows toward areas of low pressure. The molecules of air flowing past a curved surface speed up, lowering the pressure at the surface and causing the air flow to curve also. The stream of air you blow toward the bottle splits and flows around the bottle, then joins on the other side and continues to flow in a straight line. Even though it is behind the bottle, the tissue paper will blow in the wind.

WORD FILE

- **Molecules:** The smallest unit of an element or compound that still has the properties of that element or compound.
- **Pressure:** The force acting on a certain area.

Invisible Push

Blow on a piece of cardboard and it will flutter away. Right? Thanks to air pressure, the answer may not be what you think.

Materials

- 3-inch square of stiff poster board
- pencil
- large thread spool

Directions

❶ Draw a straight line from one corner to the diagonal corner on the cardboard square. Draw another diagonal line from corner to corner, creating an X.

❷ Where the two lines cross is the center of the square. Hold the thread spool in your left hand and the square in your right. Place the thread spool on the square so that the hole in the spool lines up with the center of the X. Hold the square in place with the flat of your hand.

❸ Blow down through the hole in the spool and let go with your right hand. Does the cardboard just blow away?

Action, Reaction, Results

The card tends to stay in place because the moving air creates an area of low pressure. The pressure of the air pushing up on the card is greater than the pressure pushing down on it. The card is held up by air pressure pushing against it.

Some Like it Dark

Many plants and animals have automatic responses to features of their environment, such as light, heat, gravity, odor, and water. These automatic responses are called **tropisms**. *Response to light is called phototropism.*

Materials

- long clear plastic tube with caps on each end (like a tube lamp guard, available in home supply stores)
- aluminum foil
- large jar with lid
- hammer
- nail
- tweezers
- clock or watch
- collection of small creatures from outdoor area
- lightly shaded spot

Directions

❶ Seal the openings in the caps of the plastic tube by covering them with aluminum foil. Poke a few holes in the aluminum foil.

❷ Cover half the tube with aluminum foil, so half the tube is dark inside.

❸ Get a large jar with a lid. Ask an adult to help you make 10 small holes in the lid with a hammer and nail.

❹ Use a tweezers to collect 10 small creatures from leaves, bark, and soil. They should include ladybugs, grasshoppers, larvae, snails, caterpillars, beetles, and centipedes, to name a few. As you collect the creatures, put them into the jar.

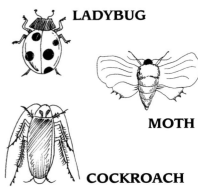

LADYBUG

MOTH

COCKROACH

❺ Remove the cap from one end of the plastic tube. Place the creatures you collected into the tube and replace the cap. Put the tube in a lightly shaded spot for 30 minutes, then check it. Are some animals in the dark part of the tube and some in the light part of the tube?

❻ Release the animals when you finish your experiment.

Action, Reaction, Results

You probably found some creatures in the dark part of the tube and others in the light part. This is because many small creatures respond differently to light. Newly hatched houseflies, or *maggots*, move *away from* light. The instinct to move into darkness helps them dig into the animal droppings they eat. Butterflies move *toward* light. This helps them find flowers for nectar and leaves on which to lay eggs.

Something Extra
Watch a fly react to temperature changes. Flies, like all insects, are cold-blooded. They cool down in cold places and heat up in warm places. To demonstrate this, get a jar with a lid. Ask an adult to help you punch holes in the lid. Put a fly in the jar and screw on the lid. Place the jar in the refrigerator for 30 minutes. Take it out and note how fast the fly moves. Now put the jar in sunlight for 30 minutes. Watch the fly move. Does the fly move faster when it is cold or warm? Release the fly when you are finished.

Fantastic Funnel

Studying creatures that live in the soil isn't easy unless you can get them to leave their natural environment. A Tullgren funnel is designed to do just that, and this experiment will show you how to make one.

Materials

- glass quart jar
- plastic funnel
- sieve with wide mesh
- soil
- lamp with flexible neck
- small jar
- magnifying glass
- insect field guide

Directions

❶ Set the plastic funnel in the quart jar.

❷ Place the sieve in the mouth of the funnel and fill it with soil from one location in your yard.

❸ Position the lamp over the sieve, but not touching it. Turn on the lamp. Wait for about an hour, then check the jar.

Experiments You Can Do in Your Backyard

❹ Move any creatures you find into a smaller jar so you can study them with the magnifying glass. Use a field guide to help you figure out what the animals are.

❺ Release the creatures back into the part of the yard where you found them.

Action, Reaction, Results

Creatures that live in the soil prefer cool, dark conditions. The warmth from the lamp drives them deeper into the soil until they fall through the sieve and into the jar. When you study the insects and other animals that you collect, count how many legs they have. Look for wings, antennae, and other body parts that can help you to identify them with the help of a field guide.

WORD FILE

- **Antennae:** A pair of long feelers on the head of certain animals such as insects.
- **Insect:** An animal with a hard outer skeleton, a three-part body, and three pairs of legs.

Ant Bait

Most ants eat dead animals and plant nectar. Some ants, however, grow fungus gardens, consume plant seeds, capture live insects, or eat other foods. But you are not likely to see those ants in your kitchen. Pharaoh ants and sugar ants are common pests in kitchens and other places where food is left out.

Materials

- anthill
- three small plastic plates
- cookie
- small piece of meat
- slice of apple

Directions

❶ Find an anthill. Make sure the ants are not fire ants. They can inflict painful stings.

❷ Prepare three small plastic plates. Put a crumbled cookie on the first plate, a small piece of meat on the second plate, and a slice of apple on the third plate.

❸ Place the three plates near the anthill. Check the plates every 15 minutes, until you see ants near them.

❹ Watch what the ants do. Do they eat one of the foods? all of the foods?

Action, Reaction, Results

Common ants probably ate all three kinds of food: sweets, meat, and fruit. Some kinds of ants, however, may have preferred one type of food over another.

Something Extra

People often use poisonous chemicals, called insecticides, to get rid of ants. Some natural substances also repel, or drive away, ants. To test some common substances, obtain one or more of the following: mint leaves, bay leaves, cinnamon, sand, talcum powder, and chili powder. Make a small circle on the driveway or sidewalk with the substance you're testing. Place an ant in the circle. Does the ant walk out of the circle? If not, the substance repels the ant. Try other household substances to see if they work. Release the ants when you finish your experiments.

Wild Webs

Spiders are among the world's smallest predators, and they have a unique way of catching their prey. They use the web as a trap. Here's a way to gather, study, and display a unique collection of spider webs.

Materials

- can of clear spray lacquer (available in hardware stores)
- 8-inch-square sheet of stiff black paper

Directions

❶ Look around your yard or a nearby park for a spider web. Touch the center of the web lightly with a leaf to be sure that the weaver is no longer around. If the spider is on or near the web, don't disturb the spider or the web. Find a web with no spider.

❷ Spray the web with lacquer several times, allowing it to dry between applications.

❸ Spray the web once again. While the web is still wet, hold the black paper up against it and lift the web onto the paper. Gently pull away any support strands.

❹ Spray the web and paper with one more layer of lacquer and allow it to dry.

❺ Follow the same procedure with other webs. Look for different sizes and shapes.

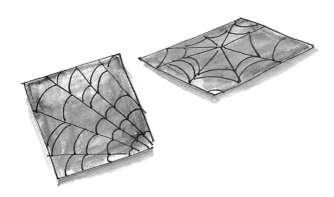

WORD FILE

- **Predator:** An animal that kills and eats other animals.
- **Prey:** An animal used by a predator as food.

Something Extra

Many spiders weave a new web every day. Some eat the old web. To find out the habits of the creature that spun the web you have collected, check in a field guide to spiders.

Along Came a Spider

How does a spider know when it has captured its prey? If you are curious about spiders and insects, try this experiment in animal behavior.

Materials

- an occupied garden spiderweb
- tuning fork (Perhaps you can borrow one from your music teacher!)
- small block of wood

Directions

❶ Explore your garden or a nearby park until you find a spiderweb with a spider in it.

❷ Hold the tuning fork by the handle and tap it against the wood block. The fork will start to hum.

❸ Place one prong of the fork against a strand of the web. What does the spider do?

Action, Reaction, Results

A spider's web is a trap the creature builds to capture its prey. When an insect becomes tangled in the sticky strands, it struggles to free itself, sending vibrations along the strands to the spider's hiding place. The tuning fork vibrates at the same frequency as the vibrations of the wings of some insects. Thinking it has captured a meal, the spider races toward the tuning fork to capture its prey.

Something Extra

Frequency is the number of times something happens during a certain time period. In the case of the tuning fork, the frequency is the number of cycles of a sound wave per second. Tuning forks can have different frequencies. If you have more than one available to you, try the experiment with each of them. Which frequency is most attractive to the spider?

Free, Fresh Air

The next time you take a deep breath, thank a plant. Much of the oxygen in the air we breath is provided by plants as a by-product of their food-making process.

Materials

- glass quart jar
- freshly picked plant leaf (such as a geranium or pothos)
- water

Directions

❶ Fill the jar with water.

❷ Drop the leaf into the water. Place the jar in a sunny location.

❸ Check the jar after one hour. Is the leaf covered with tiny bubbles?

Action, Reaction, Results

Plants use sunlight, air, and water to make their own food. The process is called photosynthesis. One of the by-products of photosynthesis is oxygen, which is released into the air through the stomata on a plant's leaves. The bubbles you see in this experiment are bubbles of oxygen.

WORD FILE

- **By-product:** A secondary product made during a process designed to produce a main product.

- **Stomata:** Tiny pores in the stems and undersides of the leaves of plants. Stomata take in certain gases such as carbon dioxide and release other gases and water vapor.

Dinner Guests

Sometimes it seems that snails will eat anything and everything in the garden. With close observation, you can discover what these hungry creatures like best.

Materials

- empty aquarium or large glass jar
- black construction paper
- paper towels
- aluminum foil
- several small rocks
- sample foods such as lettuce and other garden leaves
- 2 or 3 garden snails (found in cool, moist areas)
- cheesecloth
- string
- scissors

Directions

❶ To prepare a habitat for your snails in an aquarium or large glass jar, first cover the bottom of the area with black construction paper.

❷ Moisten a paper towel, crumple it, and place it in a corner of the habitat. Put it on a square of aluminum foil so that it doesn't dampen the construction paper. Be sure to keep the paper towel very moist as long as the snails are in the habitat.

❸ Place small rocks around the edges of the habitat for the snails to crawl on.

❹ Put a different food source in each corner of the habitat.

❺ Cover the opening with cheesecloth and tie it on with string.

❻ Observe the snails' behavior for 2 or 3 days to find out what they prefer to eat. Even if you don't see them munching, you can see which type of food is disappearing. The snails leave another clue . . . a telltale trail of slime. Remember to keep the paper towel moist.

❼ After a few days, release the snails in a cool, moist area.

Action, Reaction, Results

Snails belong to a large group of mollusks called gastropods. Gastropod means "stomach-foot." The name comes from the fact that they glide along on a large single "foot" that appears to be under the stomach of the creature. Land snails such as the common brown garden snail make a shiny trail of slime that helps them to move over surfaces more easily. Many snails, including the garden snail, eat plant matter with a raspy "tongue" called a radula.

WORD FILE

- **Habitat:** A place where a plant or animal lives.
- **Mollusk:** A group of soft-bodied animals without a backbone. Many mollusks are protected by a hard shell and live either in water or damp places.

Keeping Track

Many of the Earth's creatures have become extinct, but some have left behind traces in the form of fossils. You can get an idea of how fossils form by making some of your own.

Materials

- 2 margarine containers
- clay
- cooking spray
- small seashell
- plaster of paris
- water

Directions

❶ Flatten a $\frac{1}{2}$-inch-deep layer of clay in the bottom of a margarine container. Spray the layer with cooking spray.

❷ Press the seashell into the clay, then remove it to leave a deep impression.

❸ In another margarine container, mix $\frac{1}{2}$ cup of plaster of paris according to package directions. Pour the mixture over the clay, covering it completely. Allow the plaster to dry for about 30 minutes.

❹ Pop the finished piece out of the container. Carefully peel off the clay and observe your homemade fossil.

Action, Reaction, Results

The impression you made is an example of a kind of trace fossil. For example, an animal such as a dinosaur may have walked on the banks of a stream, leaving its footprints behind in the same way that the shell left an impression in the clay. If the footprint simply dried and hardened, it would be preserved as a cast fossil. Another possibility is that the stream may have flooded, filling the prints with mud in the same way that the plaster of paris filled the impression in the clay. Once the mud dried, the result would be a mold fossil.

WORD FILE

- **Trace fossil:** Fossil evidence left behind by living things. Trace fossils may be footprints, droppings, or impressions of plants or animals.

Something Extra

If you find an interesting animal track in the dirt, you can preserve it by using plaster of paris. Make a circle of a long, thin strip of cardboard held in place with a paper clip or tape. Push the circle into the soil around the track, then pour the plaster of paris inside the circle. Lift the hardened plaster when it dries.

The Better To See You With

If you want to get a closer look at some small object in nature, a drop of water can help.

Materials

- 8-inch piece of flexible wire
- pencil
- water

Directions

❶ Loop one end of the wire around the pencil. Twist the end to form a closed circle. Slip the pencil out.

❷ Dip the loop horizontally into a water source, such as a pond, stream, swimming pool, or water bucket to capture a drop of water.

❸ Observe any small object through the water drop. Does it appear slightly larger?

Action, Reaction, Results

The water drop becomes a simple lens. Light rays passing through the outwardly curved, or convex, water drop are brought to a focus at one point, which causes objects viewed through the drop to appear larger.

WORD FILE

- **Convex:** Outwardly curved. The opposite is concave, or inwardly curved.
- **Lens:** A piece of curved, transparent material, usually glass or plastic.

Something Extra
The lens of the eye is convex. Sometimes it may be slightly misshapen, making it hard to see properly either up close or at a distance. The corrective lenses in eyeglasses make up for the problem.

Direction Reflection

The wind direction at ground level can be affected by landforms, trees, and buildings. To help you get a better picture of which way the wind is blowing, you can make a nephoscope.

Materials

- 8-inch-square sheet of stiff white paper
- marker
- mirror 6 inches in diameter
- compass
- day with fluffy clouds

Directions

1 Mark the top edge of the paper with the letter "N" for north. Mark the left edge "W" for west, the right edge "E" for east, and the bottom edge "S" for south.

2 On a day that has fluffy clouds in the sky, place the paper on a flat surface outside. Use a compass to find north and position the paper so that the "N" is to the north.

3 Place the mirror in the center of the paper. Look into the mirror and observe the clouds. Are they moving? From what direction?

Action, Reaction, Results

As you watch the clouds in your nephoscope, you can determine which direction they are being blown by the wind. This gives you information about the wind direction. The wind is named for the direction the wind is blowing from. For example, a north wind will make the clouds move from north to south across the nephoscope.

WORD FILE

- **Clouds:** Tiny droplets of water or ice crystals that gather together in the sky.
- **Diameter:** A straight line from one side of a circle to the other side.

Any Way the Wind Blows

Do you ever wonder about the weather? This wind sock can be one of the tools to help you keep track of the weather in a backyard weather station.

Materials

- broom handle or tall stick
- 16 inches of stiff wire
- pliers
- six 12-inch pieces of lightweight string
- scissors
- single stocking or one leg from a pair of panty hose
- compass

Directions

❶ Secure the broom handle or stick in the ground so that it stands up straight and will not tip over.

❷ Create a loop with the stiff wire and use the pliers to twist the ends together.

❸ Use the scissors to poke six evenly spaced holes near the open end of the stocking. Place the open end of the stocking over the wire. Thread one end of each string through a hole and around the wire, then tie it in place.

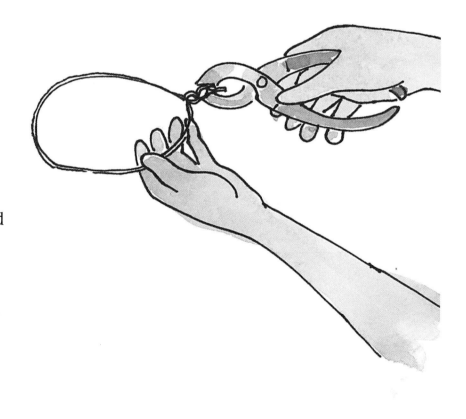

❹ Once all six of the strings have been tied, gather the loose ends together and tie them to the top end of the stick.

❺ When the wind is blowing, use the compass to determine the direction that the sock opening is facing.

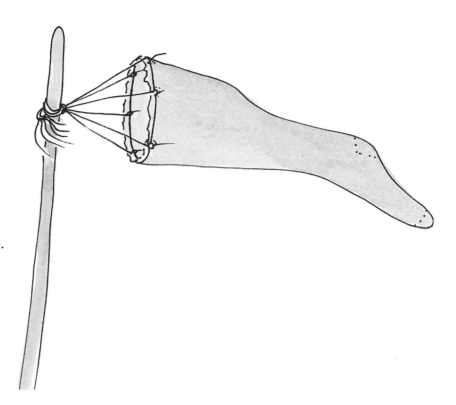

Action, Reaction, Results

The wind blows into the open end of the sock. The toe points in the direction that the wind is blowing. The direction that the opening is facing names the wind. Wind blowing from north to south is called a north wind. You can tell how strong the wind is by how straight the wind sock is.

Something Extra
Wind direction is very important to people who fly planes and sail boats. You will often see wind socks at airports and seaports.

The Air Down Under

When your feet feel good you may feel like you are walking on air. In fact, even though you are firmly on the ground, there is some air beneath your feet.

Materials

- 1 cup of water that has been boiled and allowed to cool
- glass quart jar
- 1 cup of dry soil

Directions

❶ Pour the soil into the clean quart jar.

❷ Slowly pour the water over the soil, covering it completely.

❸ Place the jar on a flat surface and observe from the side. Do you see small bubbles rising from the soil through the water?

Action, Reaction, Results

Soil is made up of many different materials, including tiny grains of rock, some finer than others. These grains do not fit together perfectly, so there are spaces in between. Air is trapped in the spaces. When you pour water into the jar, it fills the spaces and forces the air out in the form of bubbles.

Soil's Secret

The soil beneath your feet may feel very firm, but you don't have to go far to find the water in it.

Materials

- coffee can
- black construction paper
- tape
- trowel
- garden soil
- glass plate

Directions

❶ Cover the outside of the coffee can with black construction paper and tape it in place.

❷ Fill the can to within 2 inches of the edge with soil from your garden.

❸ Cover the top of the can with the glass plate and place it in a sunny location for 2 hours. Check the bottom of the plate for moisture.

Action, Reaction, Results

You will find some moisture in most types of soil. In this experiment, the warmth of the sun causes the water in your soil sample to evaporate, then condense on the plate. Try different types of soil to see which contains the most moisture.

WORD FILE

- **Condense:** To change from a vapor state to a liquid state or a more solid state.
- **Evaporate:** To convert, or change, into vapor.

Wonderful Water

Plants need sunlight, air, water, and soil to grow. Will they still grow if you leave out the soil? Give it a try.

Materials

- pebbles
- shallow baking dish
- water
- 3 clay flower pots
- peat moss
- flower seeds
- liquid plant food
- spray bottle

Directions

❶ In a sunny window, place a layer of pebbles in the baking dish. Fill each pot with peat moss and set the pots on the pebbles.

❷ Scatter several seeds in each pot, then press down the peat moss.

❸ Fill the baking dish with water. The water level should be even with the bottom of the pots. Using the spray bottle filled with water, moisten the peat moss so that it is damp but not soaked.

Experiments You Can Do in Your Backyard

❹ Check the water level in the baking dish every day, and fill to the bottom of the pots when necessary. Spray the peat moss so that it remains moist.

❺ When the seeds germinate, once a week add liquid plant food to the spray bottle according to directions on the plant food.

Action, Reaction, Results

Plants need certain things to grow. They use sunlight, water, and air to make their own food through photosynthesis. Plants also need minerals that they usually get from the soil. Peat moss holds water well, but it doesn't have the same nutrients as soil. By using liquid plant food in the water, you provide the minerals they need.

WORD FILE

- **Germinate:** To sprout a new plant from a seed.
- **Hydroponics:** The science of growing plants without soil.
- **Peat moss:** A material that forms from partially decayed plant matter that grows in bogs. It is the first stage that plant matter goes through in the process of becoming coal. Because it holds water well, it is often used to improve soil.
- **Soil:** A layer of earth that is made of weathered rock and mineral particles mixed with dead plant matter and other natural materials. Topsoil, or the upper layer of soil, is usually full of nutrients that help plants thrive.

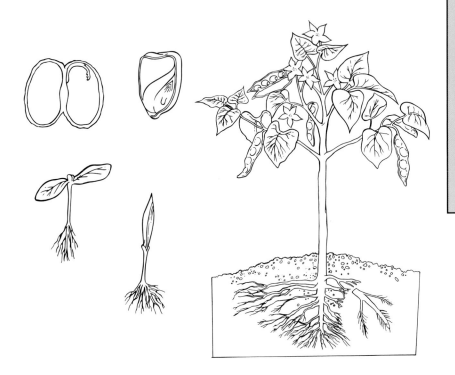

No Sweat

Some days feel dry and crisp. Others feel damp and muggy. The difference is due to differences in the humidity. You can build your own simple psychrometer to tell whether the humidity is high or low.

Materials

- 2 standard weather thermometers
- gauze
- rubber band
- glass quart jar
- water

Directions

❶ Wrap the base of one thermometer in several layers of gauze. Secure the gauze with a rubber band.

❷ Fill the jar with water. Place the gauze-wrapped thermometer in the jar so that the bulb is submerged.

❸ Place the jar and the other thermometer outside in an area out of direct sunlight. Wait 15 minutes, then compare the temperatures between the two thermometers.

❹ Keep water in the jar and compare the temperatures daily.

Action, Reaction, Results

Humidity is measured by comparing the temperature between the two thermometers. The temperature of the wet thermometer will always be lower than the dry one. The greater the difference between the two, the lower the humidity.

WORD FILE

- **Humidity:** The amount of water vapor in the air.

Down with Detergents

People use detergents to clean many things—everything from clothes and dishes to cars. Dishwashing liquid is a common household detergent. You might be surprised to find that in the wrong places, detergent has a downside.

Materials

- water
- large bowl
- waxed paper
- self-sealing plastic sandwich bag
- dishwashing liquid

Directions

❶ Fill the bowl with water.

❷ Crumple a large piece of waxed paper and stuff it into the sandwich bag. Seal the bag.

❸ Float the bag on top of the water. Add several big squirts of dishwashing liquid to the water and observe. Does the bag begin to sink?

Action, Reaction, Results

One reason that the bag floats on the surface of the water is because it has an oily coating that makes it water repellent. Detergent in the dishwashing liquid breaks up the oily coating, and the bag begins to sink.

WORD FILE

- **Detergent:** A chemical substance used to remove dirt, oil, and grease from other materials.

Something Extra

If detergents enter a natural water supply, they can cause harm to wildlife. For example, water birds rely on their water repellent feathers to float, and detergents can make their feathers less water repellent. When hiking or camping, it is important not to use detergents in or near lakes, rivers, ponds, or streams.

Tea Garden

If there is a tea drinker in your family, you have the fixings for a minigarden in every leftover tea bag.

Materials

- water
- paper towel
- small dish
- 3 used tea bags
- flower seeds (pansy seeds work well)
- spray bottle
- scissors

Directions

❶ Wet the paper towel, fold it in half, and lay it on the dish.

❷ Soak the used tea bags, then lay them on top of the towel.

❸ Using the scissors, make a hole in the center of the tea bags and poke a seed or two inside each bag.

❹ Place the dish in a warm, sunny location. Check it every day. Mist the tea bags and towel with water to keep them damp, but not soaking wet. One or more plants should sprout within 2 weeks. When the plants are about 2 inches high, plant the tea bags directly into garden soil.

Action, Reaction, Results

As long as it is kept warm and moist, a seed can germinate. Much of what a new plant needs to survive is in the seed. When nutrients in the seed are used up, the tiny plant can get food from the tea bag. Tea is made from the leaves of a plant, and the leaves contain important nutrients.

WORD FILE

- **Germinate:** To start to grow.
- **Nutrient:** A substance used to feed a living organism.

A Change In the Weather

Have you ever made plans to do something outside, only to have to change your plans because of unexpected bad weather? Other instruments you might use in a backyard weather station mostly help you observe the weather, but this barometer will help you predict upcoming changes.

Materials

- balloon
- scissors
- glass quart jar
- rubber band
- plastic straw
- glue
- 3- by 5-inch card
- marker
- tape

Directions

1. Cut a piece of balloon large enough to fit loosely over the top of the jar. Secure it in place with a rubber band.

2. Cut a piece of straw 6 inches long. Glue one end of the straw horizontally to the center of the balloon material. Place the jar on a flat surface in a sheltered area near a wall.

3. Holding the card lengthwise, write "HIGH" on the top and "LOW" on the bottom. Draw a horizontal line across the middle. Tape the card to the wall so that the straw is centered exactly on the line between the two words.

4. Check your barometer regularly, once a day. Does the straw move? If the straw is above the line, the weather is likely to be clear. If it is below the line, cloudy or stormy weather is in store.

Action, Reaction, Results

A barometer is used to measure air pressure and to predict changes in the weather. When air pressure is high the air pushes down on the balloon causing the straw to move above the line. When the air pressure is low, the straw will move below the line. High pressure usually indicates clear, stable weather. Low pressure indicates a storm or change.

A Recipe for Dirt

Not all soil is the same. Some soils hold water and dry out slowly, and others drain and dry out quickly. Knowing the type of soil you have can help you make your garden grow better.

Materials

- trowel
- 3 glass pint jars with lids
- 3 stick-on labels
- water
- marker
- notebook
- soil
- kitchen bulb siphon or turkey baster
- magnifying glass

Directions

❶ Fill each jar with 2 inches of soil. Collect each sample from a different part of your neighborhood. Label each jar and write where the sample came from. In your notebook, jot down information about the types of plants and any animals that lived in the sample area.

❷ Fill each jar with water, put on the lid, and shake until the soil is mixed. Leave the jars undisturbed for an hour or until all of the soil has settled. Note which jar settled first. Look for layers.

❸ Siphon out as much water as you can from each jar. Without shaking or disturbing the soil, set the jars in a sunny spot with the lids off so that the water will evaporate. Once the soil is dry, use the magnifying glass to examine the differences between the layers.

Action, Reaction, Results

Soil is formed from many elements including weathered rock and minerals. The type of soil it is depends on the original rock, climate, rainfall, and even the plants in the area. In this experiment, the soil becomes mixed with water, and as it settles, the heavier elements settle first and the lighter ones settle last forming layers. There are four basic kinds of soil: clay, sand, silt, and loam. Clay is the heaviest; loam is the lightest.

WORD FILE

- **Clay:** Extremely fine soil that resists drainage. Clay is the heaviest of the four soil types.
- **Loam:** Soil that is a mixture of plant matter, sand, silt, and clay soils.
- **Sand:** Grainy soil that drains quickly, made up of bits of bits of rock, minerals, and broken shell.
- **Silt:** Sandy soil that is very fine-grained.

Down the Drain

The rain forest is filled with lush plants, so you might think that it has nutrient-rich soil. In fact, rain forest soil has few nutrients. This experiment demonstrates one reason why.

Materials

- funnel
- 4 coffee filters
- glass quart jar
- 1 cup of soil
- $\frac{1}{2}$ teaspoon of powdered green paint (available at art supply stores)
- tap water
- measuring cup
- 4 plastic glasses

Directions

1. Place a coffee filter in the funnel and set the funnel on top of the glass jar.

2. Fill the filter with soil and mix in the powdered paint.

3. Pour $\frac{3}{4}$ cup of tap water through the soil. Once the water has drained through, pour it from the jar into a plastic glass.

4. Repeat step 3 three more times. Is the colored water in each glass the same shade of green?

Action, Reaction, Results

In this experiment, the green paint represents nutrients in the soil. The water represents the rain from a downpour. Each time it "rains," "nutrients" are washed away. If you continue to pour water through the soil, all of the nutrients (represented by green paint) will eventually drain away and the water will be clear.

WORD FILE

- **Nutrients:** Substances that provide food for a living thing.
- **Rain forest:** An evergreen forest that has abundant rainfall throughout the year.

Earthworks

Have you ever seen a natural cave, one that wasn't man-made? Natural caves can form in different ways, but limestone caves are carved out through the erosive action of water.

Materials

- water
- glass pint jar
- vinegar
- school chalk

Directions

❶ Fill the jar halfway with water, then finish filling it with vinegar.

❷ Place the chalk in the water-vinegar solution.

❸ Allow the jar to remain undisturbed for 30 minutes.

Action, Reaction, Results

In this experiment, the chalk you use is a form of limestone. Limestone is a sedimentary rock formed on shallow seabeds. It is made up of calcium carbonate, mainly small particles of seashells. Limestone is comparatively soft. The water and vinegar represents rainwater, which is slightly acidic. It dissolves the chalk. A similar process happens when rainwater seeps through underground beds of limestone. Where rainwater flows and pools, it gradually dissolves areas of the limestone, and those areas become caves.

WORD FILE

- **Acidic:** Having the properties of an acid or producing an acid.
- **Erosive:** The tendency of one substance to wear away another.
- **Sedimentary rock:** Rock formed by the settling of particles that form layers and harden due to the pressure of the layers above.

Number the Stars

On a clear, dark night, the sky may appear to be filled with glittering stars. Have you ever wondered how many? It would take too long to count every one, but the scientific technique in this activity will help you to estimate the number of stars glittering above you.

Materials

- 8-by-8-inch square of poster board
- ruler
- pencil
- scissors
- notebook

Directions

❶ Place the poster board on a flat surface. Measure and cut a 4-by-4-inch square from the center. You will have a square frame that is 2 inches wide on each side.

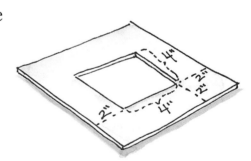

❷ Go outside and wait 5 minutes until your eyes adjust to the dark. Close one eye. Hold the frame 12 inches from your open eye and count all of the stars you can see within the square. Be sure to hold your head and hand still. Record the number in your notebook.

❸ Repeat your count in 10 different parts of the sky. Record each count in your notebook.

❹ Add up all 10 numbers, then divide by 10 to get the average number of stars per viewing. Multiply that number by 56. The result will be an estimation of the total number of stars visible in the sky with the naked eye.

Action, Reaction, Results

A square 4 inches on each side held 12 inches from your eye, gives you a view of approximately 1/56 of the celestial hemisphere. First you find the average number of stars that may be visible in the square by taking 10 different samplings, then multiply to find the total. How do you know you are seeing 1/56 at a time? At a distance of 12 inches from your eye, the total surface of the celestial hemisphere is about 905 square inches. The frame allows you to view 16 square inches at a time (905 divided by 16 = 56).

WORD FILE

- **Average:** Typical or in the middle. A mathematical average is the result of dividing the sum by the number of items added to total that sum.
- **Celestial hemisphere:** The domelike view an earthling has of the night sky.
- **Estimate:** To figure out roughly or approximately.
- **Surface area:** The measure of a surface in square units of length, such as square feet or inches.

Spinning Fountain

In the 1600s, the English scientist Sir Isaac Newton developed three laws that explain how objects move. One of these laws could be called the "I push you, you push me back" law. It says that if one object pushes on another object, the second object will push back just as hard in the opposite direction.

Materials

- empty half-gallon paper milk carton
- nail
- 2-foot-long string
- tree branch

Directions

❶ Get an empty half-gallon paper milk carton. Use a nail to punch a hole in each left-hand corner of the carton, close to the bottom (see illustration on opposite page). Punch another hole in the top flap of the carton. An adult may have to help you punch the holes.

❷ Tie one end of a 2-foot-long string through the hole in the top of the carton.

❸ Tie the free end of the string around a tree branch, so that the carton is dangling in the air.

❹ Ask two friends to cover the holes in the bottom of the carton with their fingers. Use a hose or pitcher to fill the carton with water.

❺ Ask your friends to remove their fingers from the carton. What happens when water squirts out of the holes?

Action, Reaction, Results

When water squirted out, the carton spun around. This happened because of Newton's push/push-back law. As water spurted out of the holes, it pushed back on the carton. This made the carton twirl in the opposite direction.

Something Extra
Can a balloon travel like a jet? Blow up a large balloon, but don't tie off the end. Let go of the balloon. What happens?

Putt-Putt Power

Sir Isaac Newton was one of the world's greatest scientists. He made some very important discoveries about how things move. His findings came to be known as Newton's Laws of Motion. This experiment demonstrates how the third law works.

Materials

- small plastic water bottle with cap
- scissors
- 6-inch piece of plastic straw
- clay
- tissue paper
- baking soda
- vinegar
- outdoor tub or plastic pool filled with water

Directions

❶ Ask an adult helper to use the scissors or a knife to make a hole large enough to hold the straw near one edge in the base of the bottle.

❷ Slip the straw into the hole and leave about 1 inch sticking out at the bottom. Seal the edges around the straw with clay.

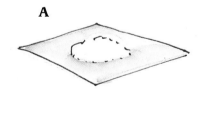
A

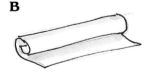
B

❸ Tear a piece of tissue about 2 inches square. (A) Place about a tablespoon of baking soda on the tissue, (B) roll the tissue to enclose the soda, (C) and twist the ends closed.

C

❹ Fill the bottle halfway with vinegar. Slip the filled tissue into the bottle and quickly put on the cap. Moving quickly, place the bottle on its side in the tub of water so that the straw is submerged. Let go and let your "boat" take off.

Action, Reaction, Results

The baking soda and vinegar combine in a chemical reaction that produces carbon dioxide gas. The gas expands inside the bottle and escapes through the straw. The gas escapes in one direction which forces the bottle in the other direction. This demonstration is an example of Newton's Third Law of Motion which states that every action has an equal and opposite reaction.

WORD FILE

- **Chemical reaction:** The interaction of two or more substances that brings about a chemical change in them.
- **Submerge:** To put a solid object in water so that it is covered.

Quick Quicksand

Can you imagine ground that looks like a solid but acts like a fluid? You don't have to imagine. With this demonstration of a non-Newtonian fluid you can create your own backyard quicksand.

Materials

- large, shallow bowl
- $1\frac{1}{2}$ cups cornstarch
- $1\frac{1}{4}$ cups water
- spoon
- $\frac{1}{2}$ cup playground sand

Directions

❶ Mix cornstarch and water in the bowl. It should be like thick mud, a little hard to stir but not dry. You may need to adjust the mixture to get the right texture.

❷ Sprinkle the surface of the mixture with playground sand.

❸ With two fingers, press lightly on the surface. Do your fingers sink easily into the mixture as they would in a fluid?

❷ Try striking it hard with your fist. Does the mixture resist like a solid?

Action, Reaction, Results

The cornstarch mixture is a non-Newtonian fluid. Fluids have a property called viscosity, or resistance to flow. A fluid with high viscosity, like honey, flows slowly. A fluid with low viscosity, like water, flows quickly. The viscosity of a non-Newtonian fluid can be changed by applying a force. In this experiment, when you press gently, you are applying little force and the fluid is less viscous. Your fingers sink in. When you hit the surface with greater force, the fluid becomes more viscous, and for a short time, acts more like a solid. Your fist meets resistance.

WORD FILE

- **Fluid:** A substance that flows and takes the shape of the container it is in.
- **Force:** Energy that can be measured by its effect. A force is anything that can stop or start an object, change its direction, or change its shape.
- **Solid:** A substance that does not flow and retains its own size and shape.

Something Extra

In this demonstration, the grains of cornstarch are suspended in water. Real quicksand is a bed of sand saturated by upwardly flowing water. The grains of sand shift and yield easily to pressure.

Let It Snow

A cold, snowy day may not seem like a good time to be outside, but it's perfect for this experiment.

Materials

- 3- by 5-inch piece of glass from a photo frame
- clear spray lacquer (available at hardware stores)
- rubber gloves
- tweezers
- magnifying glass
- refrigerator and freezer

Directions

❶ On the night before snow is predicted, place the glass in the freezer. Put the can of lacquer and tweezers in the refrigerator.

❷ Later when it's snowing, wear rubber gloves and use tweezers to remove the glass from the freezer. Using newspaper to protect anything that might get accidentally sprayed, spray a layer of lacquer on the glass. Place the glass in an open area outside where snow is falling.

❸ After about 5 minutes, move the glass to a cold but protected area. Let it remain undisturbed for 1 hour.

❹ Bring the glass inside. Use the magnifying glass to study the patterns of the snowflakes.

Action, Reaction, Results

What you see on the glass in this experiment are impressions of the snowflakes preserved in the dry lacquer. This method allows you to study the patterns even inside your warm house. Snowflakes are ice crystals that form from water vapor in clouds. The crystals take many forms, but they are always six-sided. No two snowflakes are alike.

WORD FILE

- **Crystals:** A clear solid substance with flat surfaces that meet at regular angles and form regular shapes.
- **Pattern:** A natural shape, design, or configuration.

Keeping Warm

When the temperature drops, what is the best way to stay warm? Several layers of clothing will help keep you toasty. Try this experiment to see why.

Materials

- 4 glass pint jars with lids
- stove
- water
- stick-on labels
- newspaper
- rubber bands
- towel
- box twice as large as the jar
- thermometer
- notebook
- marker

Directions

❶ Ask an adult helper to boil 4 cups of water for you. Fill each of the four jars half-full with the hot water and put on the lids. Label and number each jar.

❷ Wrap jar 1 with a thick layer of newspaper and secure it with rubber bands. Be sure to cover the top and bottom, too.

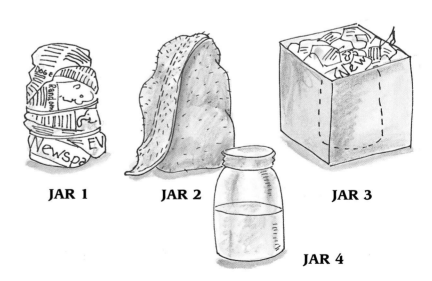

JAR 1 **JAR 2** **JAR 3**

JAR 4

❸ Wrap jar 2 completely in a towel.

❹ Place jar 3 in the box. Stuff crumpled newspaper firmly all around it. Leave jar 4 out in the open.

❺ After $\frac{1}{2}$ hour, check the temperature in each jar and write it in your notebook.

❻ Check each jar every $\frac{1}{2}$ hour until the water in each has reached room temperature. Which jar took the longest to reach room temperature?

Action, Reaction, Results

In this experiment, the jar left in the open loses heat more quickly than the others. Insulation prevents heat or cold from draining away. Some materials are good insulators and conserve heat or cold well.

Something Extra
Layers of air within or between materials improve the efficiency of the insulation. When you are going to spend time outside in cold weather, wearing layers of clothing will keep you warmer.

Earth to Star

Early sailors used an astrolabe to determine their location at sea. If you make one of your own, the stars can tell you where you are on the Earth.

Materials

- plastic protractor (from a office supply store)
- metal nut (the kind that goes on a bolt)
- pencil
- string
- scissors

Directions

❶ Measure the protractor from the flat side across to the far edge of the rounded side. Cut a piece of string double that length. Tie one end of the string to the nut. Tie the other end to the center of the flat side of the protractor.

❷ Cut two short pieces of string and use them to tie the pencil against the flat, unnumbered side of the protractor.

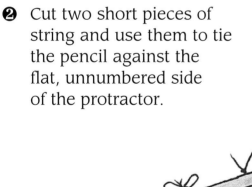

❸ On a clear night, hold the pencil up to one eye and look along it to get a good line of sight. Point the tip of the pencil at the North Star. Hold the instrument in place and look at the side of the astrolabe to get a reading. The weighted string will be in line with the number, or degree, of your latitude.

Action, Reaction, Results

People use latitude lines to figure out how far north or south they are of the equator. The protractor you used to make your astrolabe is used to measure angles. When you point the pencil at the North Star, the string measures the angle between the North Star and the horizon.

WORD FILE

- **Equator:** An imaginary line around the center of the Earth usually identified on maps.
- **Latitude:** A series of imaginary lines running east and west around the Earth and often identified on maps.

No Question North

A compass points to Earth's magnetic north pole. To find true north, or the northernmost point on Earth, all you need is a stick, a couple of rocks, and a sunny day.

Materials

- 8-inch stick or a pencil
- 2 rocks
- strong stick or nail

Directions

❶ At about nine o'clock in the morning in a sunny location, push a pencil or stick in the ground so that it stands straight up.

❷ Starting at the tip of the pencil's shadow and using the nail or strong stick, draw a circle around the pencil. Keep your circle line the same distance from the pencil as the length of the shadow. Make it as round as possible. Place a rock where the shadow touches the circle.

❸ Check your setup throughout the day. As time passes, the shadow will become shorter, then longer again. Once it touches the circle again, mark the spot with a rock. Draw a straight line to connect the two rocks.

❹ Draw a line from the pencil to the center of the line that connects the rocks. That line will point to true north.

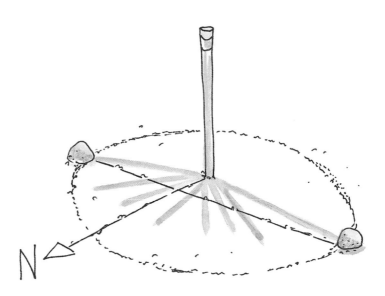

Action, Reaction, Results

The sun moves across the sky from east to west. The line you draw from rock to rock in this experiment is an east to west line. In the northern hemisphere, a line drawn from the pencil to the center of the east-west line will always point to the geographic north pole, or true north.

WORD FILE

- **Hemisphere:** Half of a round or ball-shaped object. The equator is an imaginary line that runs around the middle of the planet. The northern hemisphere is that half of the Earth that is north of the equator.

Something Extra
The magnetic poles are different from the geographic poles. The Earth is surrounded by a magnetic field, and the magnetic poles are the two points where this field comes in contact with the Earth. A compass needle points to magnetic north. After taking a compass reading, navigators adjust their findings to true north, which helps them to figure out where they are.

Fountain Fun

Create a fountain for your own backyard using warm water and air pressure.

Materials

- small plastic soda bottle with a plastic cap
- scissors
- cold water
- food coloring
- plastic straw
- clay
- small nail
- bucket or bowl large enough to hold the bottle up to the neck
- hot water

Directions

❶ Get an adult helper to use scissors or a small knife to poke a hole in the bottle cap large enough to push the straw through. Fill the bottle halfway with cold water. Add a few drops of food coloring. Put on the cap.

❷ Push the straw through the hole in the cap so that the end of the straw is about an inch from the bottom of the bottle. Surround the hole with clay to seal it.

❸ Fill the top of the straw with clay to create a plug. Use the nail to make a small hole through the clay plug.

❹ Place the bottle in a bucket or bowl. Ask an adult to fill the bucket with very hot water. Wait for a while. What happens when the water in the bottle warms up?

Action, Reaction, Results

The air in the bottle is cold, and that means that the air molecules have moved closer together. The air contracted. When you add hot water to the outer bucket, you warm the air in the bottle. The molecules move farther apart and the air expands. The expanding air pushes down on the water in the bottle and forces the water up the straw and out of the tiny opening at the top as a fine spray.

WORD FILE

- **Contract:** To squeeze down or get smaller.
- **Expand:** To spread out, swell, or get larger.

Water Loss

Take a walk around your neighborhood and you are likely to see many different kinds of plants with leaves of different shapes and textures. Does the surface and shape of a leaf have an effect on the plant? This demonstration will show one way that it does.

Materials

- 3 paper towels
- waxed paper
- 2 rubber bands
- water

Directions

❶ Wet the paper towels in water and wring them out.

❷ Spread out the first paper towel on a flat surface in a sunny area.

❸ Roll the second paper towel into a cylinder shape and place it beside the first.

❹ Roll the third paper towel into a cylinder shape and cover it completely with waxed paper. Seal the ends of the waxed paper roll with rubber bands. Place it with the other towels.

❺ After 2 hours spread each of the towels out and check for moisture.

Action, Reaction, Results

The flat paper towel is the driest, the rolled paper towel is damp inside, and the waxed-paper-covered towel is the wettest. The greater the surface area of an object, the faster the moisture in it will evaporate. That is why the flat towel dried out the fastest. The rolled up shape of the second paper towel helped it to retain moisture, while the waxy coating around the third paper towel kept it very damp.

Changing Colors

Plants need water to survive. The water must get all the way from the soil to every part of the plant. It does this through little "highways" in the stem called xylem.

Materials

- water
- 2 juice glasses
- red and blue food coloring
- fresh white carnation with a long stem
- knife

Directions

❶ Fill one glass with 2 inches of water and 10 drops of red food coloring.

❷ Fill the second glass with about 2 inches of water and 10 drops of blue food coloring.

❸ Have an adult split the stem of the carnation in the middle starting at the bottom and going up for about 3 inches.

❹ Place the glasses side by side and set the carnation in the glasses so that one part of the stem is in the red water and one part is in the blue water.

❺ Check the flower after 30 minutes have passed. Check it again after an hour.

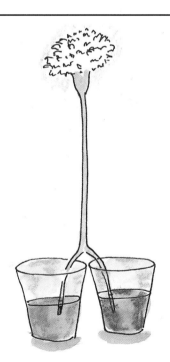

Action, Reaction, Results

The tips of the carnation petals turn colors depending on the color of the water getting to the petals. The food coloring is drawn up the stem in little tubes called xylem that usually carry water and salts from the roots up to the flowers and leaves. Even though the flower has been cut from the plant, the xylem still work. Food substances in the plant are carried from the leaves and down the stem to other parts of the plant through similar tubes called phloem.

Snip and Clip

Some lawns are long, others are kept clipped short. Is there a point at which a lawn can be mowed too short? This test will help you answer that question and find the growing point of grass.

Materials

- 3 margarine containers
- 3 saucers
- potting soil
- rye grass seed
- spray bottle of water
- marker
- ruler
- scissors

Directions

❶ Ask an adult helper to make several small holes in the bottom of each margarine container.

❷ Fill each margarine container to within $\frac{1}{2}$ inch of the rim with potting soil.

❸ Spread a small handful of grass seed evenly on the top of the soil in each container. Top each with another sprinkling of soil so that the seeds are lightly covered. Lightly mist the soil in each container with water.

❹ Label each container with a number from one to three.

❺ Place the containers on the saucers in a warm, sunny spot. Check them everyday for two weeks, and use the spray bottle to keep the soil moist.

❻ After two weeks, measure the length of the grass in each container. Using scissors, cut the grass in the first container by half. Cut the grass in the second container to within $\frac{1}{4}$ inch of the soil. Cut the grass in the third container even with the soil.

❼ Leave the containers in the same sunny location for one week and keep the soil damp. Did cutting have an effect on the grass?

Action, Reaction, Results

Most young plants have a growth point. That is the point at which new leaves are produced. If you cut away the growth point, the plant will die. Rye grass grows from a point at soil level. It can be cropped very short and still survive.

Going Green

As they ripen, tomatoes turn from green to red—unless something stops the ripening process.

Materials

- pot
- hot water
- a tomato plant with fully developed but unripe fruit
- waterproof marker
- pot holders
- brick

Directions

❶ Carefully fill the pot halfway with very hot tap water.

❷ Choose one tomato on the plant that is full grown but still green. With the marker, write a number or letter on the tomato so you can identify it.

❸ Using pot holders, position the pot under the tomato. Gently raise the pot up so that the tomato is covered by water. Prop the brick underneath the pot to keep it in place for 5 minutes.

❹ Observe the tomato over the next few weeks. Does it ripen? Do the untreated tomatoes ripen?

Action, Reaction, Results

Certain kinds of fruit ripen because of a gas called ethylene. An enzyme within the tomato produces the gas. When you dunk the tomato in hot water, you destroy the enzyme without causing any harm to the plant or the other tomatoes. Only the heat-treated fruit fails to ripen.

Something Extra

Did the heat actually kill the tomato? Cut the fruit in half and remove a few seeds. Line the inside of a glass jar with blotting paper. Stuff paper towels into the middle of the jar and add water until the blotting paper is damp but not soaked. Slip the seeds between the glass and the blotting paper, then set the jar in a sunny spot. Keep the paper moist and observe the seeds over a few days to see if they sprout.

Reach for the Light

Plants need light to grow. In this experiment, you will see what great lengths a plant will go to reach light.

Materials

- shoe box with lid
- scissors
- cardboard
- tape
- small, climbing, potted plant (such as a pothos or potato plant) that will fit in the shoe box

Directions

❶ Stand the shoe box on one short side so that the length of the box is vertical. Cut a 2-inch hole in the top of the box.

❷ From the cardboard cut two square shelves that are as deep as the shoebox, but $1\frac{1}{2}$ inches less wide. Cut 2-inch-wide strips of cardboard to use as shelf braces. Tape the braces and shelves in the box as shown.

❸ Place the box in a sunny location. Make sure the hole is on top. Set the potted plant inside, then close the box with the lid.

❹ Check the plant every evening for two weeks and water when necessary to keep it moist but not wet. Remember to replace the lid. Does the plant show an unusual growing pattern?

Action, Reaction, Results

Plants need light to fuel the process of photosynthesis. In this experiment, the plant is kept in darkness with one source of light. It grows around the barriers and toward the light.

WORD FILE

- **Phototropism:** The tendency of plant stems to curve so that leaves can grow toward the light. The tendency of plant roots to grow downward is called geotropism.

- **Photosynthesis:** The process in which plants produce their own food from sunlight, air, and water.

Something Extra
To encourage houseplants to grow evenly, it is occasionally necessary to rotate them away from the light source a little at a time.

Washing Away

Erosion is the wearing away of rocks and soil by water. In this experiment you will test how plants affect the erosion process.

Materials

- three shallow baking pans
- 2 cups pebbles
- 2 cups soil
- newspaper
- four books (each about 1 inch thick)
- leaves, twigs, and grass
- 2 cups water
- colander

Directions

❶ Fill two baking pans with pebbles, then cover the pebbles with soil.

❷ Place the third baking pan on a flat surface covered with newspaper. Stack two books at each end of the pan. Lean the two soil-filled pans against the books so they tilt downward into the third pan.

❸ In one of the soil-filled pans, cover the soil completely with a layer of leaves, twigs, and grass.

❹ Pour 1 cup water through the colander into the pan with the leafy layer. Observe what happens.

❺ Pour 1 cup water through the colander into the pan with just soil and pebbles. What happens this time?

Action, Reaction, Results

Rainwater can quickly wash away unprotected soil because there is nothing to anchor it in place. Plants, grass, leaves, and twigs keep soil from eroding by shielding it and anchoring it in place. Much of the soil from the pan without the leafy layer is likely to have washed into the spillover pan.

Dig Deep

This experiment in biodegradable materials is fun. That is, if you don't mind doing a little digging.

Materials

- an area of ground where you can dig
- disposable baby diaper, newspaper, plastic soda bottle, banana, and raw egg
- shovel or hand trowel
- five popsicle or craft sticks
- waterproof marker
- water

Directions

❶ Get permission to dig several small holes in your yard or in a vacant lot. If you have a dog that might dig up your work, pick a protected area.

❷ Gather the listed items. You can add other items to the list if you like. Dig a hole at least 6 inches deep for each.

❸ Place one item in each hole and cover the holes with soil. Write the name of each item on a Popsicle or craft stick to use as a label.

❹ Water the holes occasionally over the next 30 days. At the end of the month, dig up the items to see what condition they are in.

Action, Reaction, Results

Some materials are biodegradable. That means that as they are acted on by elements in the environment, they break down and disappear over time. The elements that act on them include water and living organisms such as worms and bacteria. The banana, the egg, and the newspaper are likely to break down easily. Some baby diapers are biodegradable; others take a long time to fall apart. The plastic soda bottle will remain unchanged.

Something Extra

Biodegradable items break down more easily in certain conditions. To test what works best, fold four sheets of newspaper into four separate squares. Bury one about 3 inches deep in dry soil and keep it dry. Bury another about 3 inches deep in damp soil, and water the soil every day. Place the third newspaper square in a pail of water. Be sure that the paper is submerged throughout the experiment. Place the last square in a dry spot exposed to direct sunlight. After 30 days, check each sample. Which has broken down the most?

Sandy Swing

*A **pendulum** is a hanging object that's free to swing back and forth. The swinging weight in a grandfather clock is a pendulum. It helps the clock keep time. The period of a pendulum is the time it takes the hanging object to make one full swing along an arc, or curve—from one end to the other and back.*

Materials

- paper cup
- hole punch
- string
- scissors
- ruler

Directions

❶ Get a paper cup. Punch three evenly spaced holes just below the rim of the cup.

❷ Measure and cut three pieces of string, each about 8 inches long.

❸ Tie the ends of the strings to the holes in the cup, one string to each hole.

❹ Tie the free ends of the three strings into a single knot.

❺ Measure and cut a 3-foot-long piece of string. Tie one end of it to the knot.

❻ Tie the free end of the string to the middle of a long, low-hanging tree branch. The string and cup form your free-swinging pendulum.

❼ Fill the cup with sand.

❽ Start the pendulum swinging back and forth. Use a stopwatch to time the pendulum for 10 full swings from one end to the other and back.

⑨ Divide the result by 10 to find the period of the pendulum. For example, if it takes 20 seconds for the pendulum to make 10 full swings, the period of the pendulum is 20÷10, or 2 seconds. Write down the result.

⑩ Repeat steps 7 and 8, but push the pendulum harder this time, so it swings over a longer arc. Repeat step 9 and record the result.

⑪ Remove half the sand from the cup and repeat steps 7, 8, and 9. Was the period of the pendulum different for each trial?

Action, Reaction, Results

The period of the pendulum was the same for each trial. This happened because a pendulum is not affected by the length of the arc or the heaviness of the weight.

Something Extra

Use your pendulum to make pictures. Place a large piece of paper under the pendulum. Use a pencil to punch a hole in the bottom of the cup, from the inside out. Cover the hole with your finger, and fill the cup with sand. Take your finger off the hole and start the pendulum swinging back and forth. Refill the cup with sand and swing the pendulum in various directions to see what kinds of pictures it makes.

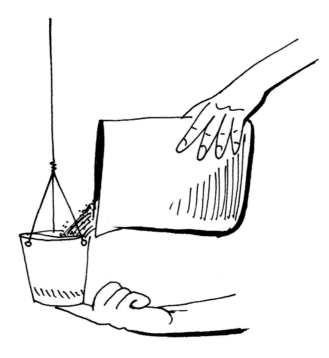

Can Contest

Send a wooden block sliding across the floor. No matter how hard you push it, the block will eventually slow down and stop. The reason is friction. Friction is a force that makes it difficult for things to move past each other. Tiny bumps on the block's surface strike tiny bumps on the floor's surface, and the block slows down. This is sliding friction. A rolling can, on the other hand, slows down and stops because both the can and floor are slightly misshapen, or warped. This is rolling friction. Friction works on things that slide, roll, or flow past each other.

Materials

- two empty aluminum cans
- pebbles
- two small pieces of aluminum foil
- two strong rubber bands
- two bricks
- wooden board, about 1 foot wide and 2 feet long
- flat area outside

Directions

❶ Get two empty aluminum cans with the tops removed. Leave one can empty. Fill the other can with pebbles.

❷ Fit a small piece of aluminum foil tightly over the top of each can. Fasten each piece of aluminum foil with a strong rubber band.

❸ Choose a flat area outside. Lay down two bricks, side by side.

❹ Rest one end of a wooden board, about 1 foot wide and 2 feet long, on top of the bricks. This will form a ramp.

❺ Hold the cans at the top of the ramp, about 2 inches apart.

⑥ Release the cans at the same time, so they roll down the ramp and onto the ground. Do the cans roll the same distance?

Action, Reaction, Results

The pebble-filled can stopped first. It did not roll as far as the empty can. Both cans were slowed down by friction as they rolled over the ramp and ground, but the pebble-filled can experienced extra friction as the tumbling pebbles rubbed against the inside of the can. This additional friction made the pebble-filled can stop sooner.

Something Extra
Use a rope to find out how friction works. Get a heavy rope, about 5 feet long. Wrap the rope around a tree once. Hold one end of the rope tightly. Ask an adult to try to yank the rope out of your hand by pulling the other end. Can the adult do it?

Whirl and Twirl

Watch an ice skater twirling. As she spins around and around, angular momentum keeps her twirling. Angular momentum depends on three things: the object's speed, mass, and distance from the center of rotation. An object that moves farther from its center of rotation slows down, and an object that moves closer speeds up. When the ice skater pulls her arms and legs in tight—so they are close to her center of rotation—she spins faster. When she lifts her arms and legs up—moving them away from the center of rotation—she slows down.

Materials

- strong 3-foot-long string
- empty thread spool
- large metal nut
- wide-open space

Directions

1 Guide a 3-foot-long string through an empty thread spool.

2 Ask an adult to help you securely tie one end of the string to a large metal nut.

3 Go outside to a wide-open space. Hold the free end of the string in one hand and the spool in the other hand. Spin the nut in a wide circle over your head. Note how fast the nut spins.

4 Slowly pull down on the string, so the nut moves toward the spool. Does the speed of the nut change?

Action, Reaction, Results

Because angular momentum stayed the same, the nut whirled faster and faster as it got closer and closer to the spool.

Something Extra

Make a hula hoop gyroscope. A gyroscope is a spinning wheel that resists changing direction as it spins. Hold a hula hoop upright on a driveway or sidewalk and give it a push. Does the hula hoop stay upright while it's rolling? What happens when it stops?

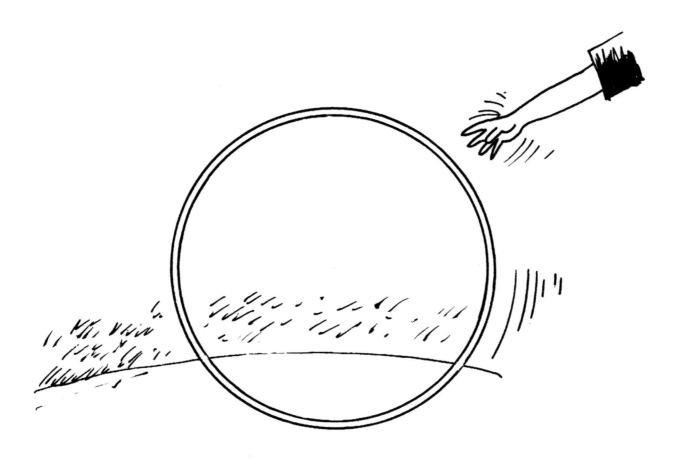

Volcano

You probably don't want a real volcano in your backyard, but you can have fun with this small, simple volcano.

Materials

- large plastic funnel with the tube cut away
- baby food jar
- clay
- baking tray
- $\frac{1}{2}$ cup hydrogen peroxide
- $\frac{1}{2}$ cup yeast
- spoon

Directions

❶ The baby food jar should fit under the upside down plastic funnel so that the opening of the jar is level with the opening of the funnel. If necessary, raise the baby food jar by putting layers of clay under it.

❷ Place the jar in the center of the baking tray. Pour the hydrogen peroxide into the jar. Moving quickly, stir in the yeast and set the funnel upside down over the jar. What happens?

Action, Reaction, Results

The combination of hydrogen peroxide and yeast produces a chemical reaction. The result is steam, foam, heat, and a hissing noise.

Something Extra

A volcano is an opening in the Earth's crust. Under certain conditions, a volcano may erupt. When it does, lava, or molten rock, gases, ash, and large rocks are noisily forced out to the surface.

Before and After

There are lots of different kinds of pollution, and some you don't have to go outside to find.

Materials

- four 3- by 5-inch index cards
- petroleum jelly
- blunt knife
- plastic bags
- vacuum cleaner
- dust rag

Directions

❶ Use the knife to spread a thin smear of petroleum jelly on two 3-by-5-inch cards.

❷ Being careful not to touch the sticky part, place one "pollution trap" on the floor in a place where it won't be disturbed. Place the other on a counter or shelf that is open to the rest of the room.

❸ After two days check the cards. Do you see dust and dirt trapped in the petroleum jelly? Place each card in a plastic bag.

❹ Vacuum your room and dust carefully, then place two new petroleum jelly-covered cards in the same positions as the first.

❺ After two days, check the cards. Are the results different?

Action, Reaction, Results

The atmosphere is filled with particles of dust and dirt that are so small they float in the air. The first two cards were exposed to a more "polluted" environment than the second two. By cleaning and vacuuming your room, you remove much of the dust and dirt that is floating around. Without special equipment it is practically impossible to remove all of the particles from the air in your room.

WORD FILE

- **Dust:** Fine, dry particles of earth or other matter.
- **Pollution:** Harmful or unpleasant substances in air, water, or soil.

Left or Right

Are you right or left handed? Can animals be right or left pawed? If you have a cat or dog, or a friend who has a cat or dog, you can find out.

Materials

- clear plastic jar (such as an empty peanut butter jar)
- pet treats
- masking tape
- cooperative pet
- notebook
- pencil

Directions

❶ Place a pet treat in the bottom of the jar.

❷ Put the jar on its side on a flat surface, such as a walkway. Tape down the jar so that it can't be rolled or tipped.

❸ Show the jar and treat to your pet. Observe which paw the pet uses to try to get the treat out of the jar. Write down your observation.

❹ Repeat the procedure eight or ten times using the same pet. Record your observations. Reward your pet with a treat for trying.

❺ Try the experiment with other pets. Record your observations. Remember to reward the pets.

Action, Reaction, Results

People tend to favor the use of one hand over another. Most humans are right-handed. Other than the fact that objects are often designed for use with the right hand, there is little benefit of one handedness over the other. Though individuals vary, most animals don't seem to have the same preferences when they try to get the treat. They are often as likely to use the left paw as the right paw to get to a treat.

WORD FILE

- **Handedness:** A tendency to use one hand rather than the other.

On Target

Hitting a moving target can be difficult. In this experiment, you'll try to hit a target that is standing still while you are moving.

Materials

- old sock
- sand
- flat rock

Directions

❶ Partially fill the sock with sand and tie a knot in it.

❷ Place the rock on the ground for a target. Stand about 20 feet from the target.

❸ Hold the sock out to one side and run as fast as you can past the target. Try to drop the sock directly on the target as you pass.

Action, Reaction, Results

The sock does not drop down in a straight line. Because you are moving when you drop the sock, it has some forward motion, or momentum. It falls in a curved path and lands in front of the target.

WORD FILE

- **Momentum:** The force produced by a moving body.

Rain Rates

A backyard weather station wouldn't be complete without a rain gauge. A simple rain gauge will help you keep track of how much rain each storm brings. Over time you can figure out the rainiest months of the year.

Materials

- trowel
- glass quart jar
- large styrofoam meat tray (such as the size used for chicken)
- scissors
- funnel with the same diameter as the opening of the jar
- ruler
- notebook
- pencil

Directions

❶ In an open area free from overhanging plants or other obstructions where it's okay to dig, dig a hole as deep as the jar is high but wide enough so the jar can be easily moved in and out.

❷ Place the jar in the hole. The neck of the jar should be even with the soil level.

❸ Cover the opening to the hole with the styrofoam tray. Cut a hole in the center of the tray just large enough to fit the funnel spout. Stick the spout through the hole.

❹ Check the jar at the same time every 24 hours for a month. Take the jar out of the hole. If there is any collected water, use the ruler to measure in inches how deep it is. Record the amount in your notebook, dump out the water, then replace the jar, tray, and funnel.

Action, Reaction, Results

This simple rain gauge does not measure actual rainfall in inches. It is a way of comparing total rainfall over days or months. Over time, you can predict a pattern. A standard rain gauge is an instrument with an open-topped container that has been calibrated (filled with fluid, measured, and marked) so the amount of rain that falls into it can be accurately measured.

WORD FILE

- **Funnel:** An object used to pour a substance into a narrow-necked container. It has a wide mouth at the top and a narrow spout at the bottom.
- **Gauge:** A measuring instrument.

Hair and Humidity

Even when it isn't raining out, the air is not completely dry. There is always some water vapor, the gas form of water. Humidity is the amount of water vapor in the air. When the air holds a large amount of water vapor, the humidity is high. When the air holds a small amount of water vapor, the humidity is low. Wood and hair soak up water vapor. That's why wooden doors swell and hair droops on humid days. A hygrometer is an instrument used to measure humidity.

Materials

- scissors
- cardboard
- nail
- pushpin
- Styrofoam block, about 9 inches high
- tape
- a long human hair
- permanent marker
- outdoor location for hygrometer

Directions

❶ Use a scissors to cut a narrow strip of cardboard, with a pointed end. Make it about 3 inches long. This will be your pointer.

❷ Ask an adult to help you make a hole in the wide end of the pointer with a nail.

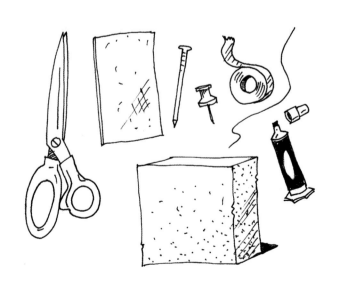

❸ Put a pushpin through the hole in the pointer and loosely attach it to an upright Styrofoam block, as shown in the illustration. The pointer should be able to move up and down slightly.

❹ Tape one end of a long human hair to the pointer, near the pushpin.

❺ Arrange the pointer so that it's horizontal, and tape the free end of the hair to the top of the block. The hair should be pulling slightly on the pointer.

❻ Make a line at the tip of the pointer, and mark it with the date. Make additional lines above and below the tip of the pointer. This device is your hair hygrometer.

❼ Put the hygrometer outside, in a place where it won't be disturbed.

❽ Check the hygrometer for 2 weeks. What does the pointer do on a humid day? What does the pointer do on a dry day?

Action, Reaction, Results

The pointer moved down on a humid day and up on a dry day. On a humid day, the hair absorbed water. This made it expand and become longer, so the pointer moved down. When the weather became dry again, the hair lost water. This made it contract and become shorter, so the pointer moved up.

Something Extra

Can you find the dew point? Warm air can hold more water vapor than cold air. When air cools at night, water vapor comes together to form droplets, called dew. Here's how to find the dew point temperature, or the temperature at which dew forms: Half fill a shiny aluminum can with water, and insert an outdoor thermometer. Add ice slowly, stirring constantly with a spoon. Note the temperature at which the outside of the can gets foggy. This is the dew point temperature.

Bubbling Rock

If you are a rock collector, this experiment is perfect for you! Use this procedure to determine the carbonate content in rock.

Materials

- rocks
- water
- metal nail file
- eyedropper
- white vinegar

Directions

❶ Gather a few rocks from outside. Try to find a variety by looking in different areas. Rinse the rocks in plain water and dry them.

❷ Make a slightly rough patch on each rock by rubbing the surface with a metal nail file.

❸ With the eyedropper, place 1 drop of vinegar on the rough patch of each rock. Observe the reaction on each rock.

Action, Reaction, Results

Certain rocks are made up of the remains of tiny shelled sea creatures called carbonates. When carbonates come in contact with a weak acid such as vinegar, it creates a chemical reaction that produces carbon dioxide gas. If you see a little bubbling when you test a rock, then it probably contains carbonates. Other rocks should not have any reaction to the vinegar.

Don't Crowd Me

Plants generally grow best when they're not too close together. Seeds of baby lima beans, for example, should be planted 6 inches apart; seeds of large sunflowers should be planted $2\frac{1}{2}$ feet apart.

Materials

- five medium-size flowerpots, 6 to 8 inches across
- potting soil
- 40 sunflower seeds
- permanent marker
- watering can
- water
- sunny spot

Directions

❶ Fill five medium-size flowerpots with potting soil.

❷ Plant sunflower seeds within the top inch of soil in each pot, as follows: 1 seed in the first pot, 3 seeds in the second pot, 6 seeds in the third pot, 10 seeds in the fourth pot, and 20 seeds in the fifth pot. Try to spread the seeds evenly in each pot.

❸ Use a permanent marker to label each pot with the number of seeds it contains. For example, write "1 seed" on the first pot, "3 seeds" on the second pot, and so on.

❹ Put the pots in a sunny spot.

❺ Fill a watering can with water, and wet the soil in each pot thoroughly. Add $\frac{1}{3}$ cup water every other day.

❻ Check the pots every few days for 8 weeks, to observe the seeds sprout and grow. In which pot do the plants seem to grow best?

Action, Reaction, Results

When the plants first sprouted, they grew at about the same rate. After 8 weeks, the sunflower plants in the "1 seed," "3 seed," and "6 seed" pots were taller and healthier than the plants in the "10 seed" and "20 seed" pots. When plants are too close together, their roots can't get enough food and water. The plants then grow poorly.

Something Extra

Create a circle of seeds. When different types of plants grow together, they may help or hurt each other. See how sunflowers and beans affect each other. Fill three medium-size flowerpots with potting soil. Within the top inch of soil, plant seeds as follows: In the first pot, plant 6 bean seeds in a circle, equally spaced. In the second pot, plant 6 sunflower seeds in a circle, equally spaced. In the third pot, alternate 3 bean seeds and 3 sunflower seeds (bean, sunflower, bean, sunflower, bean, sunflower) in a circle, equally spaced. Put the pots in a sunny spot and water them thoroughly. Add $\frac{1}{3}$ cup water every other day. Check the pots every few days for 8 weeks. Do the sunflower and bean plants grow best separately or together?

Jiminy Cricket!

This summertime experiment in animal behavior is best done on a warm evening.

Materials

- penlight
- stopwatch or watch with a second hand
- pencil and paper
- outdoor thermometer

Directions

❶ After sundown on a warm, dry summer night, sit outside where you can listen for the chirping of crickets. Use the penlight to help you see in the dark.

❷ Once you have singled out a cricket, use a stopwatch, or a watch with a second hand, to time 15 seconds. During that time, count the number of chirps your cricket makes and write the number down.

❸ Add 37 to the number.

❹ Check the temperature on the thermometer. Is the number on your paper close to the temperature?

Action, Reaction, Results

Your result may not match the temperature exactly, but it's likely to be close. Although the method is not strictly scientific, it is rooted in the science of animal behavior. Male crickets make chirping noises to attract mates. They make the noises by rubbing their forewings together. The warmer the weather, the more active these crickets become, and the more chirps per second you hear.